The Devil's Wife

Nymeria Publishing, LLC

First published in the United States of America by
Nymeria Publishing LLC, 2022

Copyright © 2022 by Will Winters

All rights reserved. Except as permitted under the U.S. Copyright Act of 1976, no part of this publication may be reproduced, distributed, or transmitted in any form or by any means, or stored in a database or retrieval system, without the prior written permission of the publisher.

Nymeria Publishing
PO Box 85981
Lexington, SC 29073

Visit our website at www.nymeriapublishing.com

ISBN 979-8-9851572-4-6

Printed in U.S.A

To Chibu, the only one who read my poetry.

Tearful Bombs

She knows evil spreads
Far outside of the boundaries of the mind
Nothing contains it.

It keeps on growing
In unknown places, no one will ever reach
She keeps on cleaning.

A polished surface
Although perfection is unattainable
There is no limit.

She's going insane
Never knowing it will never be enough
Scrubbing and washing.

Because even then
In the darkest corners of the slimmest cracks
That's where evil grows.

Diagnosed

The bright blue sky loomed over me,
Taunting me.
I stretched my neck farther,
Trying desperately to see a clip of a wing,
But only catching a feather.
The jungle was all around me,
Keeping me.
Unnatural pricks and thorns,
Rusty vines tower and searching for hours,
But no way past the horns.
Just the scorching sun above me,
Mocking me.

Turmoil

Salt filled my lungs

The invisible force dragging me under

My eyes clouded with sand

I couldn't see

And I couldn't swim

Falling and falling

farther

down

down

down

 It kept tugging on me

And I tried to get out!

Gasping for air that wasn't there

The waves bashing against my head

Blocking my

Only escape!

Only darkness

Below me

The sun clouded by a thin mirror

Only I could see through.

Urges

Fiery red ants crawled up my arms,
Their little legs poked holes into my skin,
They sharpened their teeth on my bones.

I watched as the flames spread,
Knowing there was only one way to put it out.

The ants were always whispering,
Their echos combined into a choir,
"Do it," they chanted.

I must face the heat of one thousand fires,
Or the tingle of flames from a thousand bites.

I Miss My Blue Sheets

The soft, comfy texture.

The familiar smell.

The way I sank into that ocean of blue.

That deep, sea green.

That's when I let go. That's when I sink further.

In those blue sheets.

I miss them.

Design

I often think of fabric,
Clumps of thread and string.
All stitched together,
Woven perfectly.
But sometimes the fabric rips,
Ruining the craft.
It interrupts the nature of things,
Changing up the path.
I stopped wondering where I was going,
A very long time ago.
I only know I'll end up somewhere,
And that's all I need to know.

Die In Peace

Because I've seen,
So many times,
The soul drain from,
Lifeless eyes,
I can't help but wonder,
What would it feel like?
And I've heard of,
Dying of old age,
But what does that really mean?
Do I die in peace?
And fade away,
Like going to sleep,
At the end of a day?
And if I ascended,
Would it feel like a dream?
Or would it just be black,
As all things seem?
I don't want to die,
But I want to know,
What would it be like?
Where would I go?

I Have A Crush On My Brother's Girlfriend

Aw, shit.

There she goes again,
With her cute curly hair,
And her goofy smile.

Life's not fair.

I see her with him,
And I feel green.
They're holding hands.

Why can't that be me?

I like all her pics,
On social media.
She follows me back.

Is this a dream?

He must never know.
She must never tell.
There's so much at stake but,

It's not my fault I fell.

To My Future Wife

Of all the flowers here,
You are the most radiant.

And the stars that shine above us,
Have nothing on your eyes.

And your smile is like a wave.
It washes away all doubt,

That I am in love with you,
So can you hear the ringing bells?

Shining Knight

I want to be her hero,
Her shining son of a gun.
Whisk her away on a valiant steed,
And ride into a setting sun.

I'll leap after her from rooftops!
And run across the sea.
Swing from ropes and grab her waist,
"Hold on tight to me!"

Although I can dream of courageous acts,
Reality is fleeting, I know.
Forever stuck in an unwanted body,
With a mind pecked by crows.

But just as she is not a princess,
I am no knight, you see.
And I want to be her hero,
But I know I'll never be.

Unsent Love Letter

"It's hard to explain what I feel,
To those who will never understand.
That feeling of exhilaration,
When I touch your hand.

It's like my body tenses up,
And I can hardly breathe!
You are my secret obsession,
And that's just fine with me.

And to those who don't understand,
To those who ask in dismay,
Why won't you stop messing with her?
It's just more exciting this way!

So as I watch you from a distance,
My mind begins to scheme.
Stalker is a bit harsh, isn't it?
Ha! Only in my dreams."

With love,
Unknown

Hair

I used to have beautiful brown hair.
Nice and long and thick.
But one day I cut it,
To about shoulder's length.

I thought that's what I wanted,
So I went along with it.

Later I would cut it shorter.
Eventually I would dye it blonde.
I'm not sure what happened but,
Now my beautiful brown hair is gone.

I guess that's not what I wanted,
But I went along with it.

So as I continue to grow it out,
And try to forget your face,
I realize now that what I wanted,
Was the cost of your embrace.

Turns out it's what you wanted,
And you went along anyway.

The Ice Rink

Do you remember the day we went ice skating?
That's my fondest memory of you,
Just the two of us in our romantic fantasy.
Falling together on the ice,
Holding each other to stay warm.

Do you remember when we sat down, exhausted?
And I put my arm around you,
Like I had seen so many times in the movies,
And you let me?
Oh, I wanted to kiss you!

And though I could feel eyes burn into my skin,
I didn't care because it was you, love.
You that I so foolishly pushed away.
So how could I expect you to forgive me,
When I can't even forgive myself?

Rose

I wish a girl would give me a rose,
And declare my eyes the deepest.
And gently whisper in my ear,
And tell me all her secrets.

I wish a girl would hold me close,
And kiss me lightly on my lips.
But the rose is so hard to hold sometimes,
As it pricks my fingertips.

I wish a girl would give me a rose,
And proclaim my soul the purest.
And softly kill the wrong inside,
And tell me I'm her dearest.

I wish a girl would love me so,
And promise love never ceases,
But the thorns are sharp as they rip my skin,
And petals fall in pieces.

Dear, Death

You have taken,
So many, Death.
Yet given,
So much more.
While most will feel,
Your cold hand's touch,
Some might feel,
Your warmth.
And while I know,
Your imminent grasp,
I warn you,
Stay away.
Spare the ones,
I love the most.
Spare them,
Every day.
But do not hesitate,
With me, Death.
I simply,
Cannot stay.
Dare I say,
I loathe you, Death,
But love you, All the same.

Dear, Sanity

I never really understood,

What it meant to be afraid.

Until I saw you, my love,

Slowly slip away.

For sense and thought,

I stood to reach higher.

How far I stretched my love,

But cold hands gripped you tighter.

What now is lost is gone forever,

And She shall take your place.

Henceforth, my love, I am sorry,

For I could not erase.

The Cold Bench

I've known too many people like you.
They don't want help,
But they blame others for not helping them.
They can't even help themselves so,
Why should I bother?

I tried so hard,
To make you see,
And yet you were so blind,
You could only love me,
In my dreams.

So I'll let you rot out here,
On this cold bench,
On a colder night,
Because I can't love someone,
Who refuses to love herself.

You ripped my heart to pieces,
Like it was some love letter I wrote to you.
So I hope you're reading this,
Because I don't even think you knew,
Or cared about it.

Going Mad

It is so hard pretending,
Misleading and distracting.

They know nothing, right?
Damn, I'm so bad at acting.

Spinning lies is easy,
And no web shall be had.

But I have so many secrets,
Enough to go mad.

But somehow I cannot speak,
The words that flood my mind.

But they always ask, "Robin!"
"What are you hiding this time?"

And you say it's for protection but,
Damn, this has gotten bad.

How do I keep this up forever?
Fuck, I'm going mad.

Raven-Haired Mistress

Ignore all of them,
My raven-haired mistress.
They'll never understand,
How we could be.

Sing to me,
My raven siren,
And lie and say,
You love me.

Under these stars,
Dance with me,
And pull me away,
To sea.

Drifting slowly,
Amongst these waves,
Hold me tight,
And drown me.

Dancing Alone

To me, Death is a woman,
And she is quite the Miss.
I twirl her around in her black, lacy dress,
Her beauty gaining with every spin.

I swing her and dip, swooping in for a kiss,
But she quickly turns to stop me and grins.
"Don't think me some fool," she says with delight,
As my eyes blink in innocence.

I return her smile,
With the same amount of glee.
"A fool like me?" I quip,
And she giggles, "Maybe."

I spin her some more, bringing her close,
But she pulls away, and fear gleams in my eyes.
It takes all of my strength, but I pull her in closer,
Making sure to hold on tight.

Our titillating banter goes on for a while, and finally,
I stop her where we stand.
Her eyes widen, and her smile fades, as I say,
"I want to ask for your hand."

But as we all know, Death belongs to no one,
So she leaves me to let me grow.
A moment of desperation, but she's already gone,
And I learn to dance alone.

I Hate The Sound Of My Heartbeat

I hate the sound of my heartbeat.
Like the footsteps in the distance,
It keeps me up at night.

I wish my brain would melt.
It could pour out of my ears like wax,
And spill all over the floor.

Then allow my head to feel empty.
Let my body shut down.
A useless attempt to block out the noise,

As I can still hear the thumping.
My only option is to die,
But even in death, I would still be in Hell.

Delusional Spirit

Fame is forbidden fruit.

It is offered to me by a young woman,

Who is beautiful on the outside so She,

Pretends to be sweet.

And the apple is so compelling.

Its shiny, crisp skin glows,

And I have never seen such a,

Tempting red.

I hear it calling me.

Along with the sound of the bite,

And the green cloud bursting,

Into the air.

Before I know it,

My body slumps to the ground.

Fame has taken,

Yet another soul.

Antagonist

I wonder what you think of me,

Falling short of insanity,

I'll feel guilty for eternity,

Condemned to my masculinity.

Do you know that I really miss you?

I know that I have no right to,

An apology is long overdue,

But I never really cared about you.

A toxic romance and nothing more.

Love is a sin that I adore.

My guts are painted on the floor.

A work of art you can't ignore.

You were a dream that I once had,

In a world full of nightmares; how fucking sad,

Is that? A pathetic son with no dad,

With only me to blame. I know I'm mad.

So if love is a weakness, then what am I?

A heartless monster not prepared to die.

So I steal your heart away as you cry,

"Why? You asshole, you fucking lied!"

And it's a game we play that never ends.

Over and over and over again.

You love me, but I won't give in,

And no one ever seems to win.

A Field Of Rye

There is nothing left for me here,
And nowhere left to hide.
All that's left is darkness and sadness,
And lots of wasted time.
I don't know how I got here,
As a catcher in the rye.
All I know is this empty field,
With nothing left to write.

The Devil's Proposal

"Hello, my wicked darling,
How does evil fare tonight?
Much better than your heart?
Which is more empty than mine?

I have something to offer you,
And no, it is not a rose.
So don't back away yet!
You'll want to hear what I propose.

It is only an apple,
With a shiny red glow.
Don't you hear it calling you?
Don't you want to know?

Just take one bite,
And you will soon discover,
That it will keep you warm,
Unlike your raven-haired lover.

So go ahead, don't be scared!
Let it cry out your name!
Let it shower you in love!
Let it shower you in fame!"

So Now You Know

So now you know,

As I waded through,

The bogs of confusion,

I found the swamp quite comforting,

But somehow I was still miserable,

Slowly sinking into an abyss,

And no one would ever even know,

If I died.

But I didn't die.

No, I refused to.

To die in a swamp like that,

In a pit so disgusting,

Forever chained to the very mud,

That made me.

No, I would not drown.

So now you know,

That I wanted to fly,

And as painful as it was,

I wanted to fly,

And I wanted to sing,

So I ripped my wings from those chains,

Sacrificing my feathers,

One by one,

But nothing was more painful than,

Suffocating in my own misery.

And so I wanted you to know.

So I tore my heart out of my chest,

And handed it to you as proof,

Even though I knew,

You wouldn't believe it.

So now you know,

That I soared through the air,

Like the bird I always wished to be,

Singing, "I'm free! I'm free!"

Wedding Day

Do you hear the ringing bells?
The flapping wings of doves?
Tired hooves against the ground?
A carriage meant only for love?

But love means nothing to the Devil.
No, She's much worse than me.
That's why I chose to marry Her.
So we can rule Hell for eternity.

Because He made Heaven only for men,
And I am no girl's shining knight.
So if He made me, how can I be?
A woman with no such light?

Maybe the book got it all wrong,
Because it feels good chasing desire.
Hell makes quite the lovely paradise,
As I can't burn if I like the fire.

So take these rings and seal the deal.
A bite of the apple will do.
"What do you say?" the Devil asks.
I think I'm in love with you.

Eternity

You brought me the rope,
Pushed me to the ledge,
Bound my hands and gagged my mouth,
And you helped me off the edge.
They'll say I jumped myself,
Maybe it was just for fun.
Or I might be called a victim.
Either way, I've won.
Because you guys just don't get it.
No matter how hard I have tried.
I'll never make you understand,
What you believe are lies.
But that's okay for now,
For better or for worse.
I only want to help myself,
Now that I ride the hearse.
And there's something faded over there,
In the corner of my eyes.
Never whole, a shattered soul.
Wow, I must've died.
"Here lies Robin's wicked heart."
I have been declared deceased.
They all say, in dismay,

"Forever Rest In Peace."
But I wasn't who you said I was.
And I wasn't who you wanted.
I could only be, from what it seems,
The hated and the taunted.
But they were right about something,
I will burn in Hell.
Just not for sins, it seems, I win!
Such pretty wedding bells.
And I regret I can't look down,
But I'll see you in a breath.
Now I own, upon the throne,
Fire and all death.

Acknowledgments

I want to thank Nymeria Publishing for this book. I never imagined anyone would like my poetry, let alone want to publish it. So thank you for giving me a chance. Thank you to my best friend, Chibu. You were the only one who supported me after I came out and even after I transitioned, but you were all I needed. I love you, you sexy bastard. I want to thank everyone who read this and felt connected to it because it's nice knowing that I'm not alone, as selfish as that sounds. And finally, I would like to thank myself. It was a rough couple of years, but I made it. I made it.

William Winters is a poet, writer, and author of the new poetry collection The Devil's Wife. His writing experience goes as far as writing articles for his high school newspaper. So when he dropped out of college his first year, Will felt the only thing headed for him was his parent's basement. For a long time, he felt stuck, but even if he started moving, he didn't know where to go. However, writing was his passion, constantly writing down random lines that would later turn into some of his best poetry. When he finally felt ready to come out, he slowly began his transition in late 2021.

www.ingramcontent.com/pod-product-compliance
Lightning Source LLC
LaVergne TN
LVHW041559070526
838199LV00046B/2056